THE ENERGY
DILEMMA

THE ENERGY DILEMMA

ODYSSEYS

JESSICA GUNDERSON

CREATIVE EDUCATION · CREATIVE PAPERBACKS

Published by Creative Education and Creative Paperbacks
P.O. Box 227, Mankato, Minnesota 56002
Creative Education and Creative Paperbacks are imprints of
The Creative Company
www.thecreativecompany.us

Design by Blue Design; production by Colin O'Dea
Art direction by Rita Marshall
Printed in the United States of America

Photographs by Alamy (Accent Alaska.com, Hans Blossey,
CTK, Steve Morgan, TCD/Prod.DB), Getty Images (Classen
Rafael/EyeEm, Jose Luis Stephens/EyeEm, Michele Tantussi/
Getty Images News, Santiago Urquijo/Moment), iStockphoto
(artist-unlimited, baona, DeSid, hadynyah, Mat Hanley,
IGphotography, jejim, Jennifer_Sharp, johnnorth, Mintr,
Schroptschop, svedoliver, TebNad, Suriyapong Thongsawang,
ToeyFatboy, zhongguo), Shutterstock (Rob Crandall, CL
Shebley)

Library of Congress Cataloging-in-Publication Data
Names: Gunderson, Jessica, author.
Title: The energy dilemma / Jessica Gunderson.
Series: Odysseys in the environment.
Includes index.
Summary: An in-depth study of energy, examining the effects
of fossil fuels and cleaner, more sustainable options, as well as
what people can do to limit consumption and further develop
alternative energy sources.
Identifiers: ISBN 978-1-64026-427-4 (hardcover) / ISBN 978-1-
62832-960-5 (pbk) / ISBN 978-1-64000-601-0 (eBook)
This title has been submitted for CIP processing under LCCN
2021937895.

First Edition HC 9 8 7 6 5 4 3 2 1
First Edition PBK 9 8 7 6 5 4 3 2 1

CONTENTS

Introduction

Everything human beings need to survive—air to breathe, food to eat, water to drink—is found on Earth, and on Earth alone. Yet the very planet that sustains human life has come under threat because of human activities. Rivers and lakes are drying up as people divert water for their own use. Temperatures are rising as greenhouse gases such as carbon dioxide trap heat in the **atmosphere**. Species of plants and animals are

OPPOSITE: Plants use sunlight to make nutrients out of carbon dioxide and water and produce oxygen as a byproduct in a process called photosynthesis.

disappearing as people destroy essential habitats. And the rate of many such changes appears to be accelerating. "If I had to use one word to describe the environmental state of the planet right now, I think I would say precarious," said population expert Robert Engelman. "It isn't doomed. It isn't certainly headed toward disaster. But it's in a very precarious situation right now."

Human beings' hunger for energy is only worsening the threats to the environment. We require energy for nearly everything we do, and much of this energy comes from fossil fuels such as coal, oil, and natural gas. Mining fossil fuels destroys natural landscapes and habitats, and burning fossil fuels releases greenhouse gases into the air. As the supply of fossil fuels runs low, the world is looking for more sustainable and environmentally friendly sources of energy. But in the meantime, how do we curb our appetite for energy? Are fossil fuels as harmful as some experts believe? How do we transition from fossil fuels to clean energy sources, and what will be the cost?

An Appetite for Energy

Energy is the driving force behind all human life. We use energy stored in our bodies to move, breathe, and eat. We also use energy from the earth to heat our homes, power our appliances, and run our vehicles. Much of that energy comes from fossil fuels such as coal, oil, and natural gas, which are found beneath the earth's crust. Fossil fuels are nonrenewable sources of energy, which means that they will run

OPPOSITE: Nearly two-thirds of the electricity generated in the United States in 2019 came from fossil fuels, according to the U.S. Energy Information Administration.

out someday. At the rate at which humans are using fossil fuels, scientists estimate that the world's supply could run out by the year 2125.

Although fossil fuels are being depleted quickly, they took a long time to form. They were created millions of years ago from the remains of plants and animals. As time passed, the decayed remains became buried under layers of sediment and other organic matter. The layers pressed tightly together, causing high-pressure and high-temperature conditions and turning the remains

More than three-fourths of the world's energy comes from fossil fuels. Coal-burning power plants generate electricity for home and commercial uses.

into fossils. Different types of fossil fuels were formed depending upon the type of organic matter, pressure level, and temperature involved. Coal was formed from decayed organic remains on land, while oil and natural gas were formed from decayed marine life of prehistoric seas.

Coal, natural gas, and oil contain an element called carbon, which makes them flammable. People burn these fuels to generate electricity or to power machinery and automobiles. More than three-fourths of the world's energy comes from fossil fuels. Coal-burning power plants generate electricity for home and commercial uses. Natural gas is used mostly for heating and cooking purposes. Oil is refined to make gasoline for automobiles and airplanes.

Before the mid-18th century, people used only small amounts of fossil fuels. Early civilizations often used wood for heating and cooking; after coal was found to be flammable, people began mining the material and using coal in stoves and furnaces. Kerosene, a fuel made from oil, was used in lamps. During the 17th and 18th centuries, people also relied on other sources of energy, such as wind and water. Windmills pumped water from the ground for irrigation purposes. Cotton and textile mills in Great Britain and elsewhere relied on the power of rushing water to turn large wheels that were connected to machinery inside the factories.

The Industrial Revolution, however, accelerated peo-

Promoting Sustainability

The World Energy Council (WEC), established in 1923, has members in almost 100 countries. The WEC tackles issues regarding all types of energy—coal, oil, natural gas, **nuclear**, and renewables—and is the leading energy organization in the world today. Its mission is "to promote the sustainable supply and use of energy for the greatest benefit of all people." To do so, the WEC provides reports, studies, energy-use projections, and policy recommendations to world governments, with the goal of encouraging officials to adopt energy plans that will help people reach sustainable solutions that cause the least amount of damage to the earth.

ple's use of fossil fuels. Inventors developed machines that could manufacture goods, transport people, and help perform household activities. These machines were often powered by fossil fuels. The steam engine, developed for widespread use in 1765, was one of the major contributors to the Industrial Revolution. Fueled by coal, the steam engine provided the means to power large machinery such as trains and textile looms. By the 1800s, electricity was being developed for widespread industrial use. The first power plants to distribute electricity ran on coal.

With the advancements of the Industrial Revolution came an increased demand for fossil fuels. By the 20th century, people in many parts of the world were using fossil fuels in everyday life. Automobiles, invented in 1885, and airplanes, invented in 1903, use an oil-based

Today, there are approximately 2,500 coal-fired power plants in the world. Most of the world's coal supplies are located deep underground.

fuel called gasoline. These vehicles eventually made travel faster and more accessible, enabling people to make more trips and get around with greater ease. By the 1950s, the demand for oil had grown so high that it was being pumped from every continent except Antarctica. Technology improved in the 20th century to keep pace with demand and increased people's use of electricity in the home. People could spend their time using computers, watching television, or listening to radios and stereos, all of which use electricity.

Today, there are approximately 2,500 coal-fired power plants in the world. Most of the world's coal supplies are located deep underground. Machines burrow a tunnel to reach the coal supply, or seam. Miners then ride elevators down the tunnel and use machines and other equipment to extract the coal. Sometimes coal is found closer to the surface of the ground, and coal miners use modern surface mining techniques such as strip mining or area mining. In surface mining, the ground covering the coal is removed by machines, and the coal is extracted without the use of tunnels. The coal is then transported to power plants, where it is burned to heat large vats of boiling water. The steam from the boiling water spins **turbines** that are connected to generators. The generators produce electricity, which is supplied to homes, businesses, and factories through power lines.

Oil is extracted from wells that are formed by drilling into the ground. Well pumps push the oil into pipelines,

Lasting Damage

In March 1989, the *Exxon Valdez* oil tanker ran aground in Prince William Sound, Alaska, spilling 11 million gallons (41.6 million l) of oil. The spill was not the largest in history, but it is widely believed to have been the most environmentally damaging because of the remote location, which made it difficult for cleanup workers to act quickly. More than 250,000 seabirds, 2,800 sea otters, and 300 harbor seals died from the oil's harmful effects. Hundreds of bald eagles and 22 killer whales also perished. Today, local populations of the Pacific herring and the pigeon guillemot have yet to recover.

which carry it either directly to refineries—where it is changed into substances such as gasoline, asphalt, and lubricants—or to ships, trucks, and trains, which then carry it to refineries. Natural gas, often found with oil underground, is also extracted from wells. Natural gas is piped out for use in furnaces, water heaters, and stoves.

Fossil fuels will not be available forever, but this is not the only problem with depending upon them as our primary energy source. Burning fossil fuels creates pollution and contributes to global warming. When burned, fossil fuels release carbon dioxide, a greenhouse gas, into the atmosphere. Greenhouse gases act as a blanket around Earth, keeping the planet at a temperature that can sustain life. But when the concentration of greenhouse gases becomes too high, it can cause the planet to gradually warm. Before the Industrial Revolution, there were 280 parts per million (ppm) of carbon dioxide in the air. In 2018, the amount was 407.4 ppm, according to the National Oceanic and Atmospheric Administration (NOAA). As more fossil fuels are burned, more carbon dioxide is released, which contributes to a warmer planet. Earth's average temperature has risen 1 °F (0.6 °C) over the past century, and experts expect it to continue rising. That number may seem insignificant, but even a small increase in overall temperature can have a large impact on the planet, causing catastrophic storms, droughts, and flooding.

Fossil Fuel Dependence

Today, China uses more energy than any other country in the world, and almost all of that energy is produced by fossil fuels. In 2008, global energy consumption increased by 1.4 percent from 2007 levels, with the U.S. consuming 20.4 percent of the world's total energy. China's use of energy climbed 7.2 percent from 2007 levels. However, North America, including the U.S., decreased its energy

OPPOSITE: Oil tankers transport oil around the globe; the largest ships can carry up to 2 million barrels of crude oil—enough to fill more than 5 million average-sized automobile gas tanks.

29

consumption during the same time period by 2 percent. In the U.S. alone, consumption dropped 2.8 percent, the largest decline since 1982.

By the year 2050, world energy consumption is expected to expand by 50 percent. This anticipated increase is attributed to economic growth and rising populations of the world's developing countries, such as China and India. As developing countries become developed, or industrialized, their economies grow, which usually means citizens are able to make more money. When their standard of living improves, people tend to buy their own homes and cars, which in turn increases their energy consumption.

Oil is a primary player in the energy game. Global demand for oil topped 100 million barrels per day in 2019. The U.S. consumed about one-fifth of this amount, at about 20 million barrels daily. The decrease in global consumption, the first since 1993, was chiefly caused by a widespread economic downturn and increased awareness of the costs of energy use. If this trend continues in future years, the world may see less reliance upon oil and a decline in oil prices. In 2008, the price of crude oil averaged $100 per barrel, which was a 37.7 percent increase from 2007 prices. Between 2002 and 2009, the price of oil in the U.S. nearly tripled. The price of oil dropped sharply in April 2020, plummeting to $21 per barrel, thanks to a prolonged decrease in worldwide consumption and demand.

Variation in oil prices can be attributed to many factors. One factor involves the law of supply and demand. When the demand for oil is higher than the supply, prices increase, but when the demand decreases, so do prices. In

Cleaner Coal

Because burning coal produces large amounts of carbon dioxide, chemists are continually looking for ways to make coal cleaner. One innovation in clean coal technology is called carbon capture and storage. The carbon dioxide emitted from the burned coal is captured, usually by means of chemicals that absorb the gas, before it can be released into the air. The carbon dioxide is then compressed into a liquid and piped to an underground storage unit, never to be released into the atmosphere. Scientists are also looking for ways to increase coal-fired power plants' efficiency, which will lower overall carbon dioxide emissions.

When the demand for oil is higher than the supply, prices increase, but when the demand decreases, so do prices.

the latter part of 2008, supply exceeded demand, causing the price of crude oil to decline, though the average price of oil for the whole of 2008 was still higher than that of 2007. Natural disasters can also affect oil prices, because storms, such as 2017's Hurricane Harvey, threaten oil reserves, many of which are located offshore. Wars in oil-rich countries, such as the Persian Gulf War in the early 1990s, create instability in the oil market, leading to higher oil prices.

Although oil was formed under the sea millions of years ago, many oil supplies are now located beneath land, thanks to receding oceans and movements of the earth's crust. Oil can be found in many countries, but some countries are more oil-rich than others. Most nations have to import oil to meet their energy needs, causing them to depend heavily upon those countries that supply the fuel. The 12 oil-rich countries of the Organization of Petroleum Exporting Countries (OPEC), a body that was formed in 1960, regulate oil prices and policies, controlling and protecting the business of oil exportation. Because OPEC exercises such power, the organization's actions are often open to debate. Many nations, such as the U.S., are trying to gain energy independence rather than continuing to rely on oil imports. In September 2019, the U.S. sold more petroleum than it purchased.

Coal is more abundant than oil and can be found in many parts of the world, and because it is inexpensive and widely available, consumption of coal-based energy

Disaster at Chernobyl

An accident at the Chernobyl Nuclear Power Plant in Ukraine was the worst nuclear disaster in history. In April 1986, a testing mistake led to one of the plant's reactors exploding, causing a chain of several other explosions, which emitted **radioactive** particles into the air. The radioactive cloud spread across parts of Russia (then known as the Soviet Union) and eastern Europe. More than 350,000 people were evacuated, including the entire city of Chernobyl. It is estimated that more than 125,000 people may have died from being exposed to radioactivity. The disaster raised concerns worldwide about the safety of nuclear energy and slowed its development.

China is the world's largest producer and consumer of coal, using 59 percent of the world's total supply in 2018. The U.S. uses the second-highest ..., at 13 percent.

is steadily climbing. Coal provides 28 percent of the world's total energy needs and generates 40 percent of the world's electricity. Coal is also an important ingredient in the production of steel. About 13 percent of the world's hard coal is used in the steel industry. China is the world's largest producer and consumer of coal, using 59 percent of the world's total supply in 2018. The U.S. uses the second-highest percentage of coal, at 13 percent.

While coal is the most abundant fossil fuel, it is also the dirtiest. The burning of coal releases a toxic gas called sulfur dioxide. Sulfur dioxide mixes with water in the air and causes the precipitation that falls to Earth to turn acidic. In the late 1970s and early '80s, scientists and fishers noticed a decline in animal and plant life in parts of the eastern U.S. In 1981, the National Academy of Sciences released a report that attributed that decline to acid precipitation, much of which was produced by coal-fired power plants. Acid precipitation removes nutrients from the soil and damages leaves, limiting trees' and plants' nutrient intake and making them vulnerable to diseases. Acid precipitation falling into lakes and rivers makes the water more acidic, and acidic water carries a low amount of oxygen. When fish and other marine animals cannot get enough oxygen, they suffocate and die. The U.S. Clean Air Act of 1990 called for power plants to reduce their sulfur dioxide emissions by 50 percent within 10 years. This act was a significant step

Kyoto Protocol

The Kyoto Protocol is an international treaty that calls for industrialized countries to "limit and reduce greenhouse gases emissions in accordance with agreed individual targets." The **ratification** of the Protocol by 192 countries—with the notable exception of the U.S.—has led to a near-global attempt at reducing fossil-fuel-based energy. One way a country can meet the demands of the Protocol is through emissions trading. Countries with emissions levels below the target percentage earn credits. They may then sell those credits to countries whose emissions are too high. This practice benefits countries with low emissions and the planet overall.

in reducing acid precipitation pollution in the U.S., but other coal-burning countries such as China have few policies that limit emissions from their coal-burning power plants and factories, so the pollution continues to travel around the world.

Another problem with coal-burning power plants is that they are not very efficient. At least 50 percent of the energy contained within the coal is lost when it is burned. In the U.S., the average power plant operates at only 33 percent efficiency, which means that it loses 67 percent of the energy contained in the coal. When coal is burned to boil water, it produces steam to spin the turbines, but some of the heat escapes to warm the air instead and is released through boiler chimneys. The steam that is used to spin the turbines eventually cools and is transferred to cooling towers, where it cools further and condenses into water. The warm water is then emptied into a nearby river or lake. Still more energy is lost during coal's conversion from mechanical energy (the spinning of the turbines) to electrical energy. By the time the electricity reaches people's homes, about two-thirds of the coal's energy has been lost.

Energy and the Environment

The carbon dioxide emitted from burning fossil fuels is of major concern to scientists and others around the world. Evidence points to carbon dioxide as one of the major causes of global warming. Global warming has been linked to various disastrous effects, such as major melting in the Earth's polar regions. Polar animal species, such as polar bears and penguins, that rely on cold

OPPOSITE: Research suggests that once carbon dioxide is emitted into the atmosphere, it sticks around longer than any other polluting gases produced by burning fossil fuels.

temperatures and ice and snow in order to live are being threatened by the melting of ice sheets and subsequent rising sea levels. In the north, the ice shelves and floes that polar bears walk on to reach their prey have been melting, and the gradually warming weather has caused ice to form later in the year and melt earlier. This disrupts the bears' feeding habits and causes some to die of starvation. Near the South Pole, melting snow and ice can trap penguins and keep them from moving to their feeding and breeding grounds when the seasons change.

Even without taking the melting ice into consideration, sea levels are already rising. Water expands as it warms, so warmer water covers more area than cold water, causing sea levels to rise. Warmer water also threatens many marine species that are not designed to live in warm water, so they must move to colder waters or face **extinction**. Warming oceans also affect weather patterns, causing more strong storms and hurricanes to develop. Major storms can destroy homes, lives, and habitats. In 2005, Hurricane Katrina swept through the Gulf of Mexico, killing hundreds of people and displacing thousands more who lived along the coastlines. Some believe that global warming was one of the causes behind the hurricane.

The actions of drilling and mining for fossil fuels also have negative effects on people and the environment. Underground coal mining is dangerous to the miners who must travel underground to extract the coal, as they are forced to inhale harmful gases and face the possibility of cave-ins and explosions. Many coal miners develop black lung disease from breathing coal dust, while accidents have claimed the lives of others. In 2005, an explosion

Largest Hydropower Station

The Three Gorges Dam on China's Yangtze River is the largest hydroelectric dam in the world. The dam wall is 7,660 feet (2,335 m) long and creates a reservoir 375 miles (604 km) long. Although hydroelectricity is a renewable resource, the dam project was not without controversy. About 262 square miles (679 sq km) were flooded to make the dam, requiring more than 1.2 million people to relocate and disrupting hundreds of animal species that lived in the area's ecosystems.

at the Sunjiawan mine in China killed more than 200 workers.

Surface mining techniques used to extract lignite coal (a low-grade variety of brown coal) often displace large amounts of land, disturbing both wildlife habitats and fields used for agriculture. Even though coal companies often replace the soil after the coal has been mined, it can take years for the land to return to its natural state. Mining produces large amounts of waste, which is often dumped into piles. Precipitation runs off these piles and can carry pollutants into area lakes and rivers.

With oil, most of the environmental damage can occur when the product is transported. Oil must be taken great distances to reach refineries; it crosses land on trucks, trains, and pipelines, and it is carried across oceans on large ships called oil tankers. While in transit, accidents

Harnessing Energy from Space

By 2030, Japan hopes to launch an innovative idea to capture solar energy in space. Solar panels would be placed on a satellite that orbits Earth. The panels would collect the energy and transmit it, either by waves or lasers, to a receiving station on Earth. Advantages to using such a method include the fact that solar energy is stronger in space, and the satellite could continuously capture the sun's waves—unaffected by Earth's rotations or cloud cover. Japan is not the only country considering the idea; in 2018, scientists from the California Institute of Technology created a prototype that could transmit solar energy from space.

TAKEAWAY

Oil is often called "black gold" because it is a precious resource that can bring riches to those who possess it.

can cause oil spills. One of the largest oil spills in history occurred in 1979 when two oil tankers collided in the Caribbean Sea, spilling about 316,363 tons (287,000 t) of oil and damaging marine life in the area. Seabirds coated in oil cannot fly, and they sometimes ingest the oil and die. Fish and other creaturaes in the sea are likewise poisoned by the oil. Oil spills also negatively affect the economies of nearby countries, especially those that rely on fishing and tourism.

Oil is often called "black gold" because it is a precious resource that can bring riches to those who possess it. With oil comes power and wealth, and many people want the power that oil-rich countries have. In August 1990, Iraq invaded the oil-rich country of Kuwait, with hopes of controlling its oil and acquiring its wealth. Other countries, such as the U.S. and Great Britain, concerned about their own access to Kuwait's oil, went to war against Iraq in January 1991. Kuwait was saved, but thousands of lives were lost. Many Kuwaiti oil wells were damaged from bombing in the region. After the war ended, oil fires burned for many months.

Other conflicts over oil have been waged around the world. In the African country of Nigeria, violent clashes have occurred between ethnic groups over control of the oil-abundant region around the Niger River Delta. Conflicts over oil have also arisen in the Caspian Sea republics of Kazakhstan and Chechnya, and in Southeast Asia and South America. As the demand for oil grows

Greenest and Cleanest Countries

Iceland, an island country located in the North Atlantic Ocean, is one of the "greenest" countries on the planet. Most of its electricity is generated from renewable geothermal and hydroelectric sources. Since Iceland has an abundance of volcanic areas, where heat from the earth's core lies close to the surface, residents have easy access to geothermal energy. Additionally, most homes are heated with water pumped from geothermal hot spots, while Iceland's rivers and waterfalls make it a prime candidate for hydroelectric power. Virtually the only fossil fuels used there are for powering automobiles and fishing boats, but the country has pledged to higher, more and more countries are fighting for control of the valuable resource.

Nuclear energy, which is produced by a process called nuclear fission, has been suggested as an alternative to fossil fuels because it is cleaner and more efficient. During nuclear fission, atoms of a metal called uranium are split, and small particles called neutrons are released. These neutrons bump against other atoms, splitting them and resulting in a chain reaction of nuclear fission. Fission releases heat that is used for boiling water and producing the steam that spins turbines and generates electricity. About 18 ounces (500 g) of uranium produces the same amount of heat as 1,400 tons (1,270 t) of coal. Although the U.S. leads the world in production of nuclear electricity, France, which receives about 70 percent of its power from nuclear sources, is the leader in nuclear energy consumption. Nuclear power plants release a significantly lower amount of the heat-trapping gas carbon dioxide than fossil fuel power plants do.

However, nuclear energy is not without its problems. One of the main controversies about nuclear energy revolves around the radioactive waste the power plants produce. Some waste is classified as low-level and consists of trash such as clothing, rags, and tools that have been contaminated by coming into contact with radioactive materials. Other waste is high-level and made up mostly of spent nuclear fuel, the radioactive remains of the fuel used by nuclear power plants. Exposure to radioactive waste can cause cancer, birth defects, and reproductive problems in humans. The waste remains radioactive for thousands of years, and there is no way for radioactive waste to be eliminated or recycled. Most low-level waste is stored in special, leak-proof containers and buried deep underground, while high-level waste is kept temporarily (but indefinitely) at the power plants. Apart from the wasteful byproducts, use of nuclear energy also poses a security risk. Terrorists, or people who use violence and intimidation to get the things they want, could possibly sabotage nuclear power stations to set off an explosion, or they could steal radioactive materials to make nuclear weapons and explosives.

Fueling the Future

As the problems surrounding fossil fuels become larger, most experts believe we must wean ourselves off them and begin using clean, renewable energy sources, such as hydro (water), wind, solar, and geothermal. These sources are considered clean, or green, because they do not create as much pollution or emit carbon dioxide like fossil fuels do. In 2018, 26.2 percent of the world's electricity came from such renewable

OPPOSITE: As of 2021, the U.S. Wind Turbine Database reported that almost 70,000 turbines were in operation in 44 states, plus Guam and Puerto Rico.

energy sources, but this rate is rising as the cost and consequences of using fossil fuels become higher and more apparent. Scientists, investors, and power companies are all looking toward renewable energy solutions in order to meet the world's growing energy demands.

Hydropower is already a widely used source of energy, especially when it comes to generating electricity. Flowing water contains a great amount of kinetic energy that can be harnessed to produce electricity. Dams built on rivers store water in natural or man-made reservoirs.

Algae-based Biofuel

One of the most promising biofuels of the future is algae-based. Algae are fast-growing plants that often live on the surface of ponds and lakes. The plants are rich in oils, containing about 30 times more oil than sunflower seeds, and these oils can be refined into biofuel. Another benefit of using algae for fuel is that it can be grown on nearly any body of water and does not use up land that could be used for food crops instead. In January 2009, the first airplane to use a fuel made partly from algae oils took off from a Houston, Texas, airport.

The water can be released through turbines to create electricity. Harnessing power from the ocean's tidal waves is another source of hydropower. Barriers called tidal barrages are built across **estuaries** and bays. When the tide comes in or out, water pushes through the barrages' turbines, producing electricity. Although hydropower is efficient and does not release greenhouse gases, it can damage the environment. Reservoirs created by dams flood large areas of land, destroying natural habitats. Dams change a river's natural course, flooding land and interfering with species that are native to the river. Tidal barrages often flood coastal marshes, which are feeding grounds for many seabirds, rendering the areas unusable.

The sun is a boundless source of energy that humans have only just begun to explore. Solar energy is available nearly everywhere on Earth, but it is most effective in areas that receive an abundance of steady sunshine. Solar panels, made up of a collection of solar cells that turn the sun's energy into electrical energy, can be placed on buildings or arranged on the ground. Solar cells are made of thin layers of silicon. When sunlight hits the cell, the silicon absorbs the sun's energy, and electrical charges move between the silicon layers to produce an electric current. Some problems with solar energy are that panels are expensive to install and they require coverage over a large area in order to work efficiently. According to the Center for Climate and Energy Solutions, "Solar generation (including distributed) is projected to climb from 11 percent of total U.S. renewable generation in 2017 to 48 percent by 2050, making it the fastest-growing electricity source."

The wind is another abundant energy source. In

Solar generation is projected to climb from 11 percent of total U.S. renewable generation in 2017 to 48 percent by 2050.

recent years, wind energy farms have sprung up around the world. Wind spins the blades on giant windmills, or wind turbines, turning the wind's kinetic energy into electrical energy. Windy areas of the world, such as the Great Plains region and the state of Texas in the U.S. and the Romanian province of Dobrogea, are home to the largest onshore wind farms. In Denmark, wind farms have even been built offshore, in the Baltic Sea. Wind power generates a little more than one percent of the world's energy, and that rate continues to increase. Yet although wind power may be a bountiful source of

Conserving Energy

Changing energy prices and increasing environmental concerns are causing people to think more about how they use energy today, and many individuals are becoming more energy-conscious. Instead of driving everywhere, people can conserve energy by walking or biking whenever possible. Turning off lights, appliances, and computers when they are not in use is a good way to conserve electricity, which also lowers carbon dioxide emissions. And turning down the thermostat a few degrees in winter and raising it a few degrees in summer not only lowers energy usage, but it also helps save on heating and cooling costs.

energy, it is not always a reliable one. When the wind dies down, the turbines stop spinning and no longer produce energy. To combat this problem, many wind turbines today are equipped with computerized motors that keep the turbines moving in the absence of wind.

Heat from within the earth's core can be used to create geothermal energy. In many volcanic areas, heat lies closer to the earth's surface and often produces hot springs. Steam from the hot springs can be used to turn turbines to create electricity. Another method of retrieving

Most experts believe that another way to combat the energy dilemma ... is to use alternative energy to power automobiles.

heat is to inject cold water into holes bored deep in the ground. As the water heats, it produces steam. Much care must be taken when handling geothermal energy so as to avoid mixing the water used in the process with underground freshwater supplies. Another drawback to geothermal energy is that it is not easily accessible in all countries. Iceland, which has a high concentration of volcanic areas, is rich in geothermal potential, and geothermal power heats nearly 90 percent of the country's buildings.

In addition to using clean energy for industrial and home use, most experts believe that another way to combat the energy dilemma and lessen our dependence on fossil fuels is to use alternative energy to power automobiles. Biofuels, or renewable fuel sources made from organic matter, are currently undergoing research and development. One biofuel already in widespread use is ethanol. Ethanol is made from crops such as sugar cane, sugar beets, and corn, as well as from organic wastes. Ethanol is a clean-burning fuel that is commonly blended with gasoline for use in flex-fuel automobiles, or vehicles equipped to burn both types of fuel.

Since the 1990s, engineers have been developing cars that will burn fuel more efficiently. Hybrid cars use fuel-powered engines at high speeds and electric engines at low speeds, reducing the need for gasoline and producing lower emissions. Fuel-cell cars run on battery power. The fuel-cell battery combines hydrogen

More hydrogen refueling stations have opened around the world, with most located in Iceland, Germany, and Japan in the first decade of the 21st century.

and oxygen to make electricity, which powers the motor. The only wastes produced from a fuel cell are water and negligible amounts of carbon dioxide. As fuel-cell cars have become more popular, more hydrogen refueling stations have opened around the world, with most located in Iceland, Germany, and Japan in the first decade of the 21st century.

People around the world are excited about recent innovations in clean-energy technology; however, it will take a long time to make a complete shift away from fossil fuels. Much of the rest of the world will continue to rely on fossil fuels because they are cheaper and more accessible. In addition, industries centered on fossil fuels employ millions of people, and considering that so many countries' economies rely on the export, import, mining, and burning of fossil fuels, a global shift toward clean energy is highly controversial. Even though clean energy development will eventually create more jobs, those who are currently employed or invested in the fossil fuel industries fear losing their jobs or money.

Still, many fossil-fuel-based companies are investing in alternative energy in efforts to become more energy conscious and create more jobs. For example, since 2005, oil and natural gas company British Petroleum (BP) has invested $2.9 billion in alternative energy sources such as biofuels, wind, solar, and hydrogen. Many electric companies in the U.S. and Europe offer local customers the opportunity to buy power produced by green energy instead of fossil fuels, and the trend is widening.

As the world moves toward embracing clean, renewable energy sources, the energy dilemma of the last few decades could become a thing of the past. With the help of scientists, engineers, corporations, and individuals, Earth may once again become a place of boundless energy opportunities, sustaining all life for centuries to come.

Selected Bibliography

Coal Utilization Research Council. "Clean Coal 101: What Is Clean Coal Technology?" www.coal.org/clean_coal_101/index.asp.

Darley, Julian. *High Noon for Natural Gas: The New Energy Crisis*. White River Junction, Vt.: Chelsea Green, 2004.

Elliot, David. *Energy, Society, and Environment*. 2nd ed. New York: Routledge, 2003.

Evans, Robert. *Fueling Our Future*. New York: Cambridge University Press, 2007.

Flannery, Tim. *The Weather Makers: How Man Is Changing the Climate and What It Means for Life on Earth*. New York: Atlantic Monthly Press, 2005.

Krupp, Fred, and Miriam Horn. *Earth: The Sequel; the Race to Reinvent Energy and Stop Global Warming*. New York: W. W. Norton, 2008.

World Energy Council. "About WEC: What WEC Does." http://www.worldenergy.org/about_wec/135.asp.

Worldwatch Institute. "Making Better Energy Choices." http://www.worldwatch.org/node/808.

Endnotes

atmosphere   the layer of gases that surrounds Earth

conversion   the process of changing from one form or function to another

crude oil   oil in its natural state, before it is made into gasoline and other products

developing countries   the poorest countries of the world, which are generally characterized by a lack of health care, nutrition, education, and industry; most developing countries are in Africa, Asia, and Latin America

economies   the social systems that involve production and consumption of countries' wealth, goods, and services

estuaries   the wide mouths of rivers where they join the sea

ethnic   relating to large groups of people with common racial, national, religious, or cultural backgrounds

extinction   the condition or process of a species or larger group no longer existing

Industrial Revolution   a period during the late 18th and early 19th centuries in Europe and the U.S., marked by a shift from economies based on agriculture and handicraft to ones dominated by mechanized production in factories

industrialized	having highly developed industries or manufacturing activities
irrigation	the distribution of water to land or crops to help plant growth
kinetic energy	energy produced by motion
looms	frames or machines for interlacing threads to form cloth
nuclear	having to do with energy created when atoms are split or joined together
organic	derived from or relating to living matter
radioactive	characteristic of substances such as uranium that give off particles of energy as their atoms decay; the energy is dangerous to human health
ratification	formal approval of a treaty or agreement so that it can take effect
refined	processed or changed; crude oil is refined into usable products such as gasoline and lubricants
silicon	a chemical element found in sand and rocks, often used in making electronics, glass, and cement
sustainable	using a resource in a way in which it is not depleted or permanently damaged
turbines	machines that are driven by water, steam, or a gas flowing through the blades of a wheel

Websites

JPL: Teach
https://www.jpl.nasa.gov/edu/teach/tag/search/Climate+Change

Find activities, resources, and other materials about science topics, including climate change.

NOAA: Teaching Climate
https://www.climate.gov/teaching

From videos to experiments, learn more about climate and energy.

Note: Every effort has been made to ensure that any websites listed above were active at the time of publication. However, because of the nature of the Internet, it is impossible to guarantee that these sites will remain active indefinitely or that their contents will not be altered.

Index